Word Recognition

Activity Pages
and Portfolio Record Sheets

by Mary Tarasoff

A way to focus on phonics and sight words
that supplements other reading activities

I. Phonics Patterns and Blending Sounds
II. Sight Words
III. Examples
IV. Connecting with Spelling

© Active Learning Institute 1994

These pages may be copied for the purchaser's own classroom use.

ISBN 1-895111-12-9

Published in Canada by:

Active Learning Institute
P.O. Box 6275
Victoria, B.C. V8P 5L5
Tel: (604) 477-0105
Fax: (604) 477-9105

Introduction

Some students easily learn to recognize words by sight and to decode words using phonics. However, others need more direct instruction and practice along with listening to stories, reading stories, and other language activities.

The activities in this resource book focus on phonemic awareness, blending sounds and phonics (Section I) as well as on sight words (Section II). They are meant to be a quick activity, a way to focus on these two word recognition strategies. Because these are easy to do, they can be added to a home reading program. Parents have reported that they like to do these as well as reading to or with their children.

These activities are also designed so that the student is involved in evaluating their own progress. The students themselves should highlight the words and check off the words they read, and then graph the number of words read. In this way, their progress in these activities and reading, which is usually not very evident, is made very visual.

Incorporate these activities into your language arts program along with all the other strategies you know that help children learn to read.

I. Phonics Patterns and Blending Sounds

Phonics Patterns and Blending Sounds

This activity should take only a few minutes each day and should be done as part of a lesson that involves reading literature (books, magazines, etc.). It is important that this activity of reading words is connected to other reading that the students do. These pages are only extra ways to focus attention on certain words or sounds as needed. Which phonics pattern page is used is determined by the needs you have observed as students read to you.

Before the activity, explain the purpose, relate it to the students' decoding miscues, and also discuss strategies for decoding words (e.g. sounding out, using meaning, rereading, reading on). Students also may need some extra instruction in phonemic awareness — becoming aware of the individual sounds in words — and some extra help with blending sounds together. After the activity, have the students find words with a similar pattern in the book they are reading.

Activity

Students are timed as they read words (for only 30 or 60 seconds). The number of words read is graphed. This activity focuses on increasing fluency in blending sounds together, in recognizing phonic patterns and common letter sequences, and on developing automaticity of word recognition. Students are also developing phonemic awareness of initial, medial, and final sounds. Besides the vowel patterns, these words also provide a review of the consonants, consonant digraphs, and blends.

Portfolio Progress Sheets

As well as being useful for teaching phonics and blending sounds, these sheets are records of progress which can be included in the students' portfolios.

Connecting Spelling

The word lists on these pages can also be used as a source of words follo phonic patterns. Based on the needs of your students, choose a certai relationship or spelling pattern to focus on for a while in your langua Have children find words in their own reading and writing and as the Add these words to a chart, have students spell these words on chalk "test" each other. In your teaching activities, point out the pattern bei the patterns that are more common, and those that are less commor frequently found that "aim", and "eam" is more common than " "eaf", and "eef").

A. For students just beginning to learn phonics

- Before starting this activity, students may need lessons in rhyming, blending sounds, letter-sound relationships.

- Students read the words for 30 or 60 seconds.

- Graph the number of words read in that time.

- Discuss students' skill and progress.

- Note progress over time.

- Have students find similar words/phonics patterns in other books/materials.

- When students are reading, if they need to decode an unfamiliar word, remind them of similar phonic patterns they have already learned.

- When students quickly read the words starting with the first column, have them begin at later columns, to give them practice applying their skill and phonics knowledge to other words.

Word Recognition

at	an	10	add	20	am		cap		bag
bat	can		bad		dam		lap		gag
cat	Dan		dad		ham	30	map		lag
fat	fan		fad		jam		nap		nag
mat	man		had		Pam		rap	40	rag
pat	Nan		mad		ram		sap		sag
rat	pan		pad		Sam		tap		tag
sat	ran		sad		tam				wag	50
vat	tan								
	van								

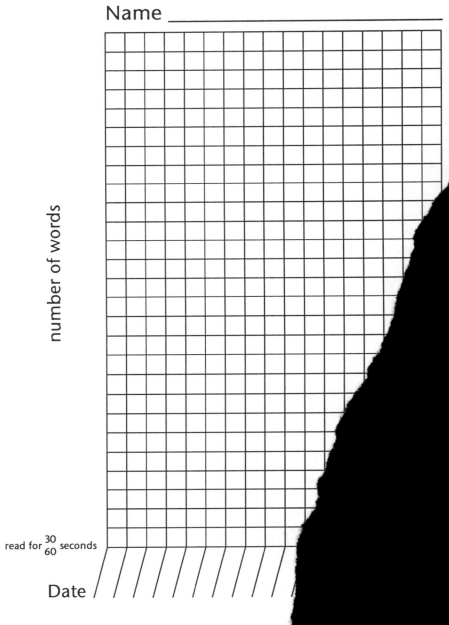

Name _____

number of words

read for $\frac{30}{60}$ seconds

Date

dot	bog		cop	odd	on	cob
got	dog	10	hop	cod	con	job
hot	fog		mop	god	Don	lob
jot	hog		pop	nod	Ron 30	mob
lot	jog		sop	pod		rob
not	log		top 20	rod		sob
pot						
rot						

Name _____

number of words

read for $\frac{30}{60}$ seconds

Date

bun	bug	but	cup	cub
run	dug	cut	pup	dub
nun	hug	gut	sup	hub
pun	jug 10	hut	gum	rub
run	lug	jut	sum	sub 30
sun	mug	nut		tub
	tug	rut 20		

Name _____

number of words

read for 30/60 seconds

Date

B.   For students who are able to rhyme and blend sounds fairly easily

- These lists are longer than those in Section A and are meant for students who have already some skill in blending sounds together and in rhyming words.

- These lists focus on the vowel patterns, but also provide an opportunity for assessing and reviewing consonants and consonant blends and digraphs.

- Some students may benefit from more direct review of the blends (see pages 30 and 31).

- See instructions at beginning of Section A for how and when to use these activity pages with students and as portfolio record sheets.

at	mad	bag	bash	flash	glass	last
bat	pad	gag	cash	brash	brass	mast
cat	sad	lag	dash	crash	grass 130	past 140
fat	clad 40	nag	hash	trash 120		blast
mat	glad	rag	lash 110	splash	ask	
pat		sag	mash		bask	bath
rat	am	tag	sash	bass	mask	math
sat	dam	wag	stash	gas	task	path
vat	ham	shag 80	smash	lass	flask	
chat 10	jam	stag	slash	mass		atch
that	Pam	slag	clash	pass	cast	
slat	ram	flag	succotash	class	fast	
scat	Sam	brag				
flat	tam	drag				
brat	slam 50					
splat	swam	cab				
	cram	dab				
an	gram	jab				
can	pram	lab				
Dan	tram	nab 90				
fan 20	scram	tab				
man	abraham	stab				
Nan	cap	slab				
pan	lap	scab				
ran	map	blab				
tan	nap 60	crab				
van	rap	grab				
than	sap					
span	tap	band				
scan	chap	hand				
clan 30	slap	land 100				
plan	snap	sand				
	clap	stand				
add	flap	gland				
bad	crap	brand				
dad	trap 20	grand				
fad	strap					
had						

Name _____

number of words

read for 30/60 seconds

Date

dot	cop ✓	cob 50	gong	fond	ball basket
got	hop	lob	long	bond 70	call 90
hot	mop	mob	pong	pond	fall
jot	pop	rob	song		hall
lot	sop	sob	thong	boss	mall
not	top	slob	strong	loss	tall
pot	chop 30	snob	prong	moss	wall
rot	shop	blob		toss	stall
shot	slop	glob	honk	floss	small
slot 10	stop			gloss	
spot	clop	bong		cross	
blot	flop	dong 60			
clot	crop				
	drop				
bog					
dog	odd				
fog	cod				
hog	god 40				
jog	nod				
log	pod				
clog 20	rod				
flog	prod				
smog	trod				
frog					
	on				
	con				
	Don				
	Ron				

Name _____

number of words

read for 30/60 seconds

Date

ant
plant
plant

catch.
patch.
snatch
batch .
hatch .
latch .
match .
watch .
dispatch

bun	but	sung	blush	dusk	stunk
fun	cut	slung	flush	musk	spunk 90
nun	gut	stung	plush	husk 80	skunk
pun	hut	swung		tusk	clunk
run	jut	flung 60	us 70		flunk
sun	nut	strung	bus	bunk	plunk
shun	rut		Gus	dunk	drunk
stun	shut 40	gush	fuss	junk	trunk
spun		hush		punk	
	gum	lush	bust	sunk	
bug 10	hum	mush	dust	chunk	
dug	rum	crush	just	slunk	
hug	tum		must		
jug	sum				
lug	slum				
mug	drum				
tug	glum				
chug	plum				
shrug	chum 50				
slug	crumb				
snug 20	dumb				
drug					
thug	bump				
cub	dump				
dub	hump				
hub	jump				
rub	lump				
sub	pump				
tub	stump				
club	slump 60				
stub 30	clump				
snub	trump				
scrub					
	hung				
	lung				
	rung				

Name _____

number of words

read for 30/60 seconds

Date

in	nil 40	bit	spit	is	ditch
bin	pill	fit	skit	his	hitch
din	quill	hit	grit	this	pitch
fin	sill	lit			rich
pin	till	mitt	dim	dish	stitch
sin	will	knit 70	him 80	fish	twitch
tin	chill	pit	Kim	wish 90	which
win	spill	quit	limb	swish	witch
thin	still	sit	Tim		
chin 10	skill	wit	whim		with 100
shin	swill 50	slit			
spin	drill				
skin	frill				
grin	grill				
	trill				
bid					
did	dip				
hid	flip				
kid	hip				
lid	lip				
quid 20	nip				
rid	rip 50				
Sid	sip				
slid	tip				
skid	whip				
	chip				
if	ship				
big	snip				
dig	slip				
fig	skip				
jig	clip				
pig 30	flip 60				
wig	drip				
	grip				
ill	trip				
bill	strip				
dill					
fill					
gill					
hill					
kill					
mill					

Name _____

number of words

read for 30/60 seconds

Date

bed
fed
led
Ned
red
Ted
wed
shed
sped
sled   10
bled
fled
bred

beg
leg
peg

el
bell
dell
fell   20
sell
tell
well
shell
spell
smell
swell

em
jem
hem   30
them

en
Ben
den
fen
men
pen
ten
when
glen   40
then

bet
debt
get
let
met
net
pet
set
wet   50

end
bend
fend
lend
mend
send
tend
wend
vend
spend   60
blend
friend

bent
cent
dent
gent
lent
pent
rent
sent   70
tent
went
vent
spent

es
guess
less
mess

best
guest   80
lest
nest
pest
quest
rest

test
vest
west
zest
chest   90
blest
crest

crept
swept
kept
slept

Name _____

number of words

read for $\frac{30}{60}$ seconds

Date

hat	kit	hid	lack	cub	tam
hate	kite	hide 50	lake	cube	tame
mat	tin	plan	tack	glad	Sid
mate	tine	plane	take 60	glade	side
rat	tap	gap	lick	glob	bit
rate	tape 30	gape	like	globe 70	bite
bad	snack	back	quit	scrap	win
bade	snake	bake	quite	scrape	wine 80
mad	stack
made 10	stake
dot	flack
dote	flake
duck	pick
duke	pike
quack	quit
quake	quite 40
pick	smock
pike	smoke
not	rod
note 20	rode
rob	rid
robe	ride
pin	mop
pine	mope

Name _____

number of words

read for $\frac{30}{60}$ seconds

Date

may	vain	ape	ate	rave	age
day	chain	drape	date 100	cave	cage
say	strain	gape	fate	Dave	page
pray	slain	grape	gate	gave	sage
tray	brain	nape	hate	pave	rage
bay	drain	rape	late	save	wage
gay	grain	tape	mate	wave	stage
hay	sprain		rate	slave	
lay		came	slate	crave	
pay 10	air	dame	skate	grave 120	
ray	fair 50	fame	crate	brave	
way	hair	game 90	grate 110		
clay	lair	lame			
slay	pair	name			
play	stair	same			
sway	chair	tame			
gray		blame			
stray	paint	flame			
	quaint	frame			
aid	saint				
laid 20	taint				
maid	dainty 60				
paid					
raid	aim				
braid	claim				
ail	ace				
bail	face				
fail	lace				
hail	mace				
jail	pace				
mail 30	race				
nail	grace				
pail	brace 70				
rail	trace				
sail	space				
tail					
wail	ade				
	fade				
train	made				
pain	wade				
stain	spade				
rain 40	blade				
	glade				
	grade 80				

Name _____

number of words

read for 30/60 seconds

Date

Pete	steep	steam	real	cheap	brief	shriek
here	cheep	dream	teal	heap	chief	tier
	sheep	cream	heal	leap	belief	pier
see	sleep	beam	deal	reap	thief	
bee	sweep	team	meal		grief	priest
fee		seam	seal	each		niece
gee	beer	stream	veal	beach 120	field	piece
knee	deer		zeal 110	teach	yield 130	
wee	cheer	clean		peach	wield	
tree	leer 50	mean	east	reach	shield	
flee 10	peer	bean 80	beast			
	steer	dean	yeast			
feed	queer	lean	feast			
deed	sneer					
need		eat				
seed	beet	meat				
weed	feet	neat				
heed	greet	treat				
greed	meet	wheat				
steed	street	pleat				
bleed	fleet 60	cheat				
	sweet	cleat 90				
leek 20	sleet	bleat				
meek	sheet					
peek		ear				
seek	pea	tear				
week	tea	near				
sleek	sea	year				
cheek	flea	dear				
		rear				
eel	read	fear				
heel	bead	gear				
peel		hear 100				
feel 30	beak 70	smear				
steel	leak	spear				
	peak					
seen	teak					
queen	weak					
green	streak					
	speak					
seem	sneak					
	squeak					
jeep	bleak					
deep	creak 80					
keep						
sweep						
peep 40						
seep						

number of words

read for $\frac{30}{60}$ seconds

Name _____

Date

ode
code
lode
mode
node
rode
strode

no
so
go   10
ho

doe
foe
hoe
Joe
roe
toe
woe

coke
joke   20
poke
woke
stoke
smoke
bloke
stroke
choke
broke
spoke

dole   30
hole
mole
pole
role
sole
vole
stole
whole

dome
home   40

bone
cone

hone
lone
tone
clone
drone
stone

cope
dope   50
hope
mope
pope
rope
grope

core
fore
gore
lore
more   60
pore
sore
tore
wore
store
spore
swore
chore

dote
note   70
rote
tote
vote

cove
dove
grove
drove
stove

oak
croak   80
cloak
soak

coal
foal

goal
shoal

roam
foam

loan
moan   80

soap

oar
soar
boar

boast
coast
roast
toast

oat
boat   90
coat
moat
bloat
float
gloat

road
load

oaf
loaf

most   100
ghost
host
post

owe
bow
low
mow
row

sow
tow   110
stow
snow
show
slow
blow
flow
glow
crow
grow
throw   120

own
mown
sown
blown
grown
flown
thrown

growth

bowl

yellow   130
fellow

willow
hollow
follow
pillow
shadow
elbow
widow
window
sparrow   140
minnow

old
bold
cold

fold
gold
hold
mold
sold
told   150
scold

bolt
colt
jolt
volt

most

Name _____

number of words

read for 30/60 seconds

Date

die	dine	bite	right	high	mild 90	sly
fie	fine	kite	sight	sigh 80	child	sty
pie	line	mite	tight 70		wild	spy
tie	mine	site 60	blight	bind		sky
	nine	rite	bright	find	by	spry
ice	pine	white	fight	kind	cry	
dice	tine	write	flight	blind	dry	
lice	wine	quite	fright	mind	fly	
mice	vine		might	wind	fry	
nice	spine 40	dive	night	grind	my	
rice 10	swine	hive	plight	hind	ply	
vice	brine	live		rind	pry 100	
slice						
spice	pipe					
thrice	ripe					
	wipe					
life	viper					
wife	snipe					
strife						
	dire					
bike	fire					
hike	hire 50					
like 20	mire					
Mike	sire					
pike	tire					
	wire					
dime	spire					
lime	squire					
mime						
time						
chime						
slime						
grime						
crime 30						

Name _____

number of words

read for $\frac{30}{60}$ seconds

Date

boon
goon
moon
loon
noon
soon
spoon
swoon
croon

balloon   10
cartoon
caccoon
raccoon
harpoon

boom
doom
room
zoom
broom
bloom   20
gloom

hoot
boot
loot
root
toot
shoot

roof
aloof
proof   30
spoof

cool
fool
pool
tool
spool
stool
school

oops
hoop   40
loop
droop
stoop
scoop

tooth
booth

mood
brood

boo
moo   50
too
zoo

choose
loose

moose
goose

new
few
dew
hew   60
pew
brew
stew
flew
drew
crew
slew   70
chew
blew
grew   70
screw

blue
clue
true
due
glue
sue

rescue
argue
avenue   80
statue

pursue
tissue
continue

use
fuse
muse
accuse
abuse

dune   90
tune

rule
mule

cube
tube

cute
lute
mute
flute

cure   100
sure

duke

huge

dupe

Name _____

number of words

read for $\frac{30}{60}$ seconds

Date

sound	ouch	loud	south	how	prowl
round	pouch	cloud	mouth	now	scowl
around	grouch	proud		cow	fowl
pound	crouch		down	bow	dowel
found	vouch 20	mouse	town	vow	towel
mound	slouch	house	gown	wow	vowel
hound		our	clown	pow 60	
bound	out	flour 40	crown 50		
wound	about	sour	drown	owl	
ground 10	pout	foul	frown	growl	
	scout	noun	brown	howl	
mount	trout				
count	doubt				
mountain	spout				
fountain	sprout				
amount	shout 30				
	snout				
	stout				
	clout				

Name _____

number of words

read for 30/60 seconds

Date

boy	enjoy	join	hoist	oil	avoid
joy	decoy	coin	joist	boil	poison
toy	employ	joint	moist	coil	anoint
coy	oyster 10	point		foil	moisture
Roy	royal		voice 20	soil	sirloin
soy	convoy		choice	toil	turmoil
			noise	spoil 30	
			poise	broil	

Name _____

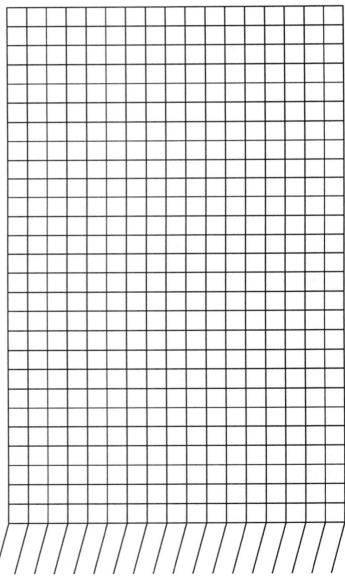

number of words

read for ${}^{15}_{30}$ seconds

Date

look	rookie	good	wool		
book	cookie	hood	woof		
took		stood			
shook	foot	wood			
cook					
hook					
nook					
rook					
brook					
crook 10					

Name _____

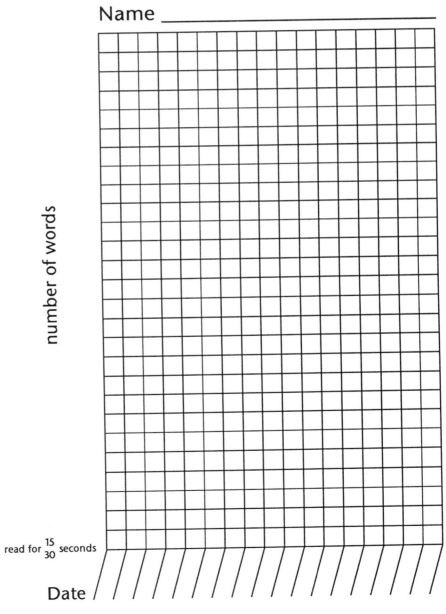

number of words

read for $\frac{15}{30}$ seconds

Date

Word Recognition

are

bar
car
far
mar
par
tar
star
scar
spar   10

bard
card
hard
lard
yard
chard

scarf
snarl

bark
dark   20
hark
lark
mark
park
stark
spark
shark

arm
farm
charm   30
alarm

barn
darn

carp
harp
tarp
sharp

art
cart
dart   40
mart
part
tart
chart
smart
start

arch
larch
march
parch   50
starch

harsh
marsh

or
for
nor

cord
ford
lord

cork   60
fork
pork
stork

form
storm

born
corn
horn
morn
torn   70
worn
thorn
scorn
sworn

port
sort
short
sport
snort   70

forth
north   80

torch
porch
scorch

Name _____

number of words

read for 15/30 seconds

Date

her

verb

herb

herd

jerk

perk

perm

term

stern

fern   10

stern

perch

father

mother

brother

sister

never

ever

under

faster   20

quicker

slower

harder

better

cleaner

charter

farmer

earl

early

pearl   30

earth

search

burr

cur

fur

purr

blur

curb

curd

curl   40

purl

hurl

lurk

surf

turf

burn

churn

turn

furnish

furnace   50

blurt

curt

hurt

church

lurch

urchin

burst

sir

fir

stir   60

girl

swirl

twirl

whirl

dirt

flirt

shirt

squirt

first

thirst   70

firm

squirm

chirp

bird

third

birch

birth

Name _____

number of words

read for 30/60 seconds

Date

law	crawl	lawn	haul	vault	autumn
paw	sprawl	prawn	Paul	sauce	author 40
saw	brawl	drawn	maul	fraud	auto
jaw	drawl	yawn			
thaw	shawl	dawn 20	haunt	pause	
raw		fawn	daunt	gauze	
draw		pawn	flaunt 30	saunter	
claw		hawk			
flaw		squawk	launch		
straw 10			haunch		

Name _____

number of words

read for 15/30 seconds

Date

stumble
bumble
rumble
grumble
crumble
humble
handle
jungle
simple
sample 10
trample
dimple
bundle
candle

bottle
cattle
middle
muddle
twiddle
tattle 20
little
kettle
ruffle
raffle
paddle

puddle
muffle
pebble
bubble
saddle 30
guzzle
drizzle
fizzle

staple
stable
table
rifle
trifle
ladle
cradle 40
able
title
fable
cable
maple

bugle
stifle
circle

vowel
towel 50
cancel
camel
hovel
funnel
tinsel
tunnel

novel
hotel
label 59

Name _____

number of words

read for $\frac{15}{30}$ seconds

Date

chant	still	snap	crust	chip
flash	spill	skin	smell	drop
thump	shell	trap	stuff	shrink
theft	class	flask	twist	blank
bunch	grip	split	grim	string
shelf	drum	sled	plush	screech
cramp	plot	blink	plant	crisp
floss	trap	trod	stamp	flint
stress	drag	thank	this	blast
scuff 10	plum 20	brand 30	those 40	shrimp 50

Name _____

number of words

read for 30/60 seconds

Date

grasp	sheep	thin	sport	than	slab
plush	wheel	chunk	bath	crash	blend
shop	then	with	bush	clip	flick
chill	church	brag	cloth	drift	snap
when	wish	strap	price	print	splint
each	prize	grand	plump	clamp	grain
strong	tramp	frame	clap	swoop	bring
grunt	frill	trunk	drink	shrimp	brim
branch	brass	drain	swim	plum	sled
shunt 10	grill 20	sneak 30	twin 40	spring 50	trod 60

Name _____

number of words

read for 30/60 seconds

Date

bud	hen	leg	gush	fall	rent
sat	dot	jam	bump	hid 50	hand
cod	wig	rap	tab	bell	trunk
hit	bill	top	spin 40	fled	cub
let	plum	nut	strong	pig	fill
red	fog	loss 30	cross	shot	west
bug	crop	slam	sped	club	mug
hop	lip 20	pit	ball	pen	sip
lid	him	pod	hung	hog	fish
sit 10	met	slug	wet	nest	then 70
had	fun	frog	crab	tap	
cut	sent	set	bunk	hill 60	

Name _____

number of words

read for $\frac{30}{60}$ seconds

Date

hope	train	time	hoop	stool	field
say	real	neat	yeast	soap	note
moon	joke	vote	foam	chew	room
tree	dine	hoe	tire	away	weed
stole	slave	hive	deal	hike	mode 60
die	tore	pool	rope	treat 50	colt
gave	boat	fry	cry 40	more	root
beak	wage	tube 30	drain	kite	bind
foe	mice 20	soon	mole	date	few
grow 10	blue	told	pine	dice	moose
right	fear	flame	leap	droop	

Name _____

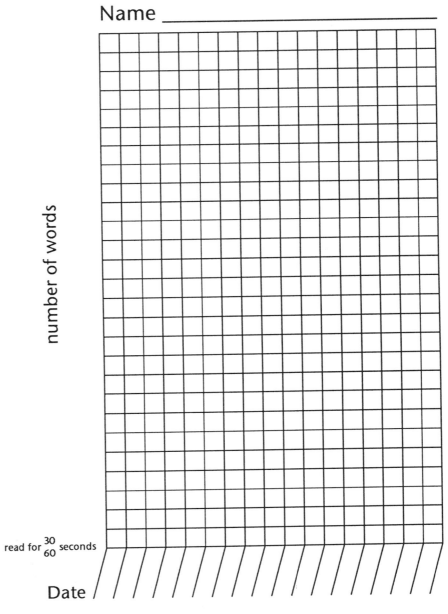

number of words

read for 30/60 seconds

Date

nine	dime	flack	choke	fire	bold
snake	find	poke	bite	peach	hate
sail	peak	track	name	hat	snipe
pin	new	own	mute	spy	spoon
drove	code	mail	cut	truck	cake
oak	bloom	quick	pie	pail	pick 80
flute	coal	seed	sight	hoot 70	quack
same	wife	slime	pair 60	meal	hike
pine	flight	grew 50	cove	tooth	
seek 10	zoo 40	snip	bike	coat	
stick	cub	cheap	say	hike	
tram					
throw					
dive					
pay					
cod					
clue					
meat					
stroke					
goal 20					
met					
slice					
late					
night					
pack					
chief					
slim					
bolt					
cube					
stair 30					

Name _____

number of words

read for $\frac{30}{60}$ seconds

Date

ground	boil	droop	choice	howl	snout
loud	vow	show	throw	tooth 50	good
boy	shoot	coin	gown	blow	how
clown	own	house	oil 40	voice	spoil
look	mood	cow	couch	now	pouch
slow	low	fool 30	took	join	toot
pool	growl	soil	grown	royal	thrown
owl	shook 20	count	mouse	bound	glow
hood	clout	avoid	cool	blown	hook
sound 10	toy	drown	crow	cloud	sprout 70
zoom	stood	cook	mount	point	enjoy
spout	frown	grow	oyster	booth 60	scoop

Name _____

number of words

read for $\frac{30}{60}$ seconds

Date

scar	skirt	thorn	earl	torn	bird
bark	for	lard	burn	blurt 50	marsh
herb	blur	curd	sharp	curb	form
harsh	spark	smart	pearl 40	lark	pork
porch	sport	fork	fir	stern	farm
jerk	church	scarf 30	starch	chum	earth
chart	dart	sort	torch	squirm	scorn
thirst	girl 20	fern	early	mark	hurt
born	forth	arm	north	hurl	firm
fur 10	search	storm	chirp	first	barn 70
hard	burst	surf	yard	bar	
perch	pearl	mark	dirt	turn 60	

Name _____

number of words

read for 30/60 seconds

Date

wall	maul	loud	walk	tall	auto
law	drawl	paw	squawk	draw	snout
flaunt	proud	spout	how	haunt	vault
cloud	sauce	pout	launch	mall	mouth
straw	brown	howl	town	prawn	also
count	talk	lawn	always	hawk	mound
dawn	sour	fraud	foul	haul	want
fault	salt	saw	stall	frown	fowl
raw	mouse	fall	sprout	pause	
hour 10	water 20	shawl 30	crawl 40	scowl 50	

Name _____

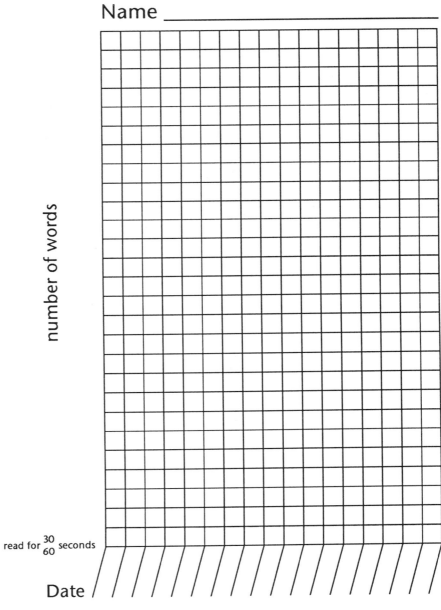

number of words

read for $\frac{30}{60}$ seconds

Date

C.   Other Activities

1. For each vowel sound, brainstorm words and categorize into spelling patterns. (Helps students to listen for and isolate sounds in words.)

2. Extend the brainstorming by finding words in reading materials. (Helps students to focus on spelling patterns and to realize phonics is useful for decoding words as well as for spelling.)

3. Categorize words by sounds and spelling patterns. (Helps students see the patterns, note which ones are most common, which ones might be tried first for decoding or spelling).

4. Teach blending of sounds directly — model how sounds are blended together, have students use letter tiles and move them together as the sounds are said. (Helps children learn to blend sounds using tactile, visual and auditory input together.)

5. Play rhyming games. Read rhymes leaving rhyming words out for students to fill in. Brainstorm rhyming words. (Helps students learn to manipulate sounds and to isolate [hear better] the vowel sounds.)

6. Have students say words without initial consonant(s) or without final consonant(s). For example, say "jump" without the "j" (ump) — what vowel is heard? Say "jump" without the "p". (Helps students isolate the sounds and hear the vowel sounds and blended letters.)

7. Have students make up sentences using words (rhyming or same vowel sound). Use these for dictation or buddy dictation activity.

8. Play vowel bingo. Students have card with several words on it with different vowel sounds. Read word or have student give word. Students cover all words with same vowel sound.

pine	jump	bed	joke	train
hope	boat	hot	file	tie
read	log	pen	meet	hand
gate	sat	cube	dog	play
must	trap	lake	pet	day

let

II. Sight Words

A. For students who are just beginning to read

B. For students who already easily recognize about 100 sight words

Instructions

Developing "sight words" — words easily and quickly recognized

1. Students read each word on the "Words I Can Read" page. They highlight words that you acknowledge as being correct and read easily (by sight, not sounded out). If they did not easily recognize a word, tell them that they will be learning it, and that they will come back to this page later to mark the ones they learn.

2. Choose words they did not easily and quickly recognize. List on the sheet "Words I am learning to read." With their help, make up sentences with these words. (Language Experience Approach)

3. Each day have them read the sentences first and then check off the words in the list that they recognize immediately.

4. After a few times (4–6), they then select new words to learn.

This activity, which takes only a few minutes, is only a part of their reading lesson. Have students read other material and also search for these words in other language activities. It is important that this activity focusing on these words occurs connected to the time when the students are reading other books/materials. This activity of reading words is one extra way to focus attention on sight words. (See examples in Section III)

A copy of the "Words I am learning to read" page can be sent home for an easy practice activity.

Note:

The "Words I am learning to read" activity page on page 48 is meant for children just beginning to learn sight words. There is more space provided for sentences ("my stories") than on page 49. Once children know quite a few sight words, and find the process easier, the activity page on page 49 can be used. Sentences can be printed beside the list. Older children can use this page also for learning to read new words and also learning to spell words they already read really easily (see also page 83).

To show progress — Portfolio Record Sheets

Students return to the original recording page "Words I Can Read" (Portfolio Record Sheet) and read the words not previously highlighted. If they are able to recognize the words immediately, they then highlight them and count the total of words they now know. This new total is graphed. These pages can be kept in the students' portfolios. (See examples in Section III)

Connecting Spelling

As students learn to read words easily, they can begin to focus on learning to spell them correctly. Words from earlier lists that they already have learned to read can become lists for spelling. Besides focusing on these words in "Word Study" times and practice at home, students should be checking their own writing for these words. Once focused on and "studied", the expectation is that they spell the words correctly in their writing. You can use the portfolio record sheets (Words I am learning to spell A through E or 1 through 6 — see Section IV) to track progress.

A.   For students who are just beginning to read

Lists based on the 200 most commonly used words

Words I Can Read — A

a	come	here	look	run	up
and	down	I	make	said	we
away	like	in	me	see	at
for	is	my	the	yellow	big
funny	it	not	three	you	blue
go	jump	one	to	yes	can
help	little	play	two	this	am
good	stop				

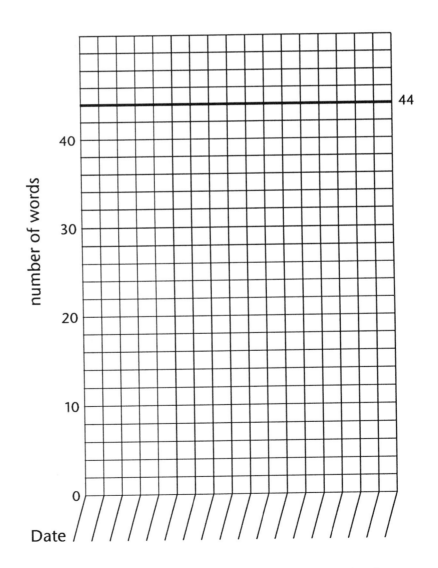

number of words

44

Date

Words I Can Read — B

all	did	must	ran	they	white
do	new	ride	who	are	eat
no	saw	too	will	ate	get
now	say	under	with	as	on
she	want	black	have	his	our
so	was	find	brown	he	out
soon	well	by	but	into	please
that	went	where	came	there	what

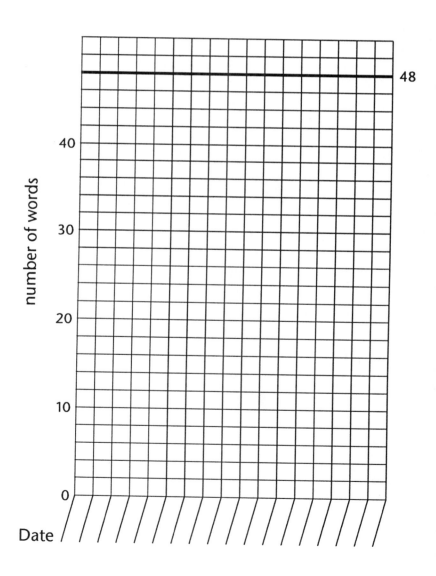

Words I Can Read — C

after	fly	her	old	take	pretty
call	thank	how	from	again	an
give	just	open	them	sit	sleep
then	over	know	going	any	or
think	put	let	had	ask	us
round	live	has	could	may	some
were	every	him	of	when	

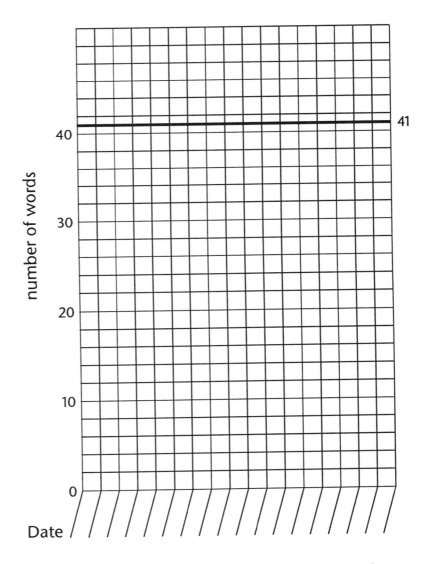

Words I Can Read — D

always	gave	pull	these	wish	those
read	goes	cold	around	work	upon
right	green	does	because	been	don't
its	sing	would	use	made	fast
before	best	many	very	your	walk
wash	tell	off	five	found	buy
got	if	their	which	once	start
pick					

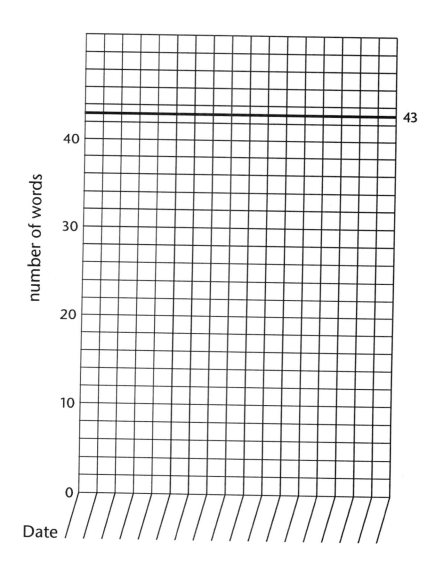

Words I Can Read — E

about	drink	hot	much	show	warm
better	eight	hurt	myself	six	write
first	small	never	fall	bring	both
only	keep	far	carry	clean	full
kind	own	ten	why	cut	laugh
today	together	seven	light	grows	done
draw	hold	long	shall	try	

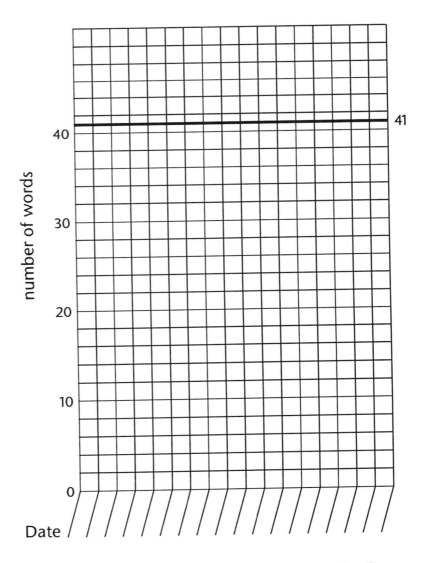

Words I am learning to read

My Stories

Name _____

Words I am learning to read

Date _____

Words I am learning to read spell

Date _____

B. For students who already easily recognize about 100 sight words

Word Recognition

Words I Can Read (1)
(115 Most Commonly Used Words)

a	about	after	all	an	and		are
as	at	be	been	big	brother		but
by	can	come	could	dad	day		did
do	does	down	each	find	first		for
from	go	had	has	have	he		her
here	him	his	how	I	if		in
into	is	it	its	just	know		like
little	long	look	love	made	make		many
may	me	mom	more	most	my		name
no	not	now	of	off	on		one
only	or	other	out	over	people		said
saw	say	see	she	sister	so		some
than	that	the	them	then	there		these
they	this	three	to	two	up		very
want	was	way	we	went	were		what
when	where	which	who	will	with		would
yes	you	your					

Words I Can Read (1)
115 Most Commonly Used Words

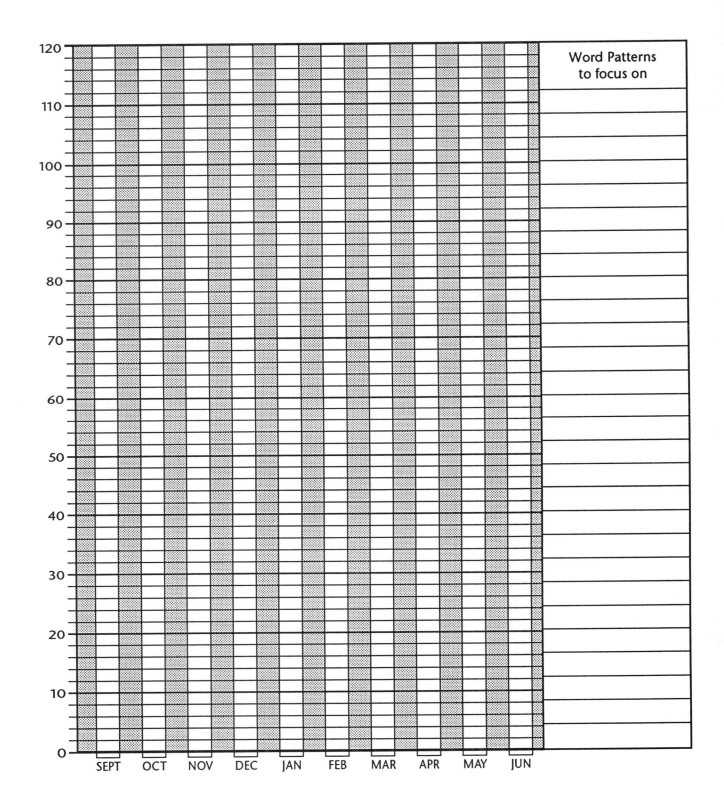

Word Patterns
to focus on

Words I Can Read (2)
Next 365 Most Commonly Used Words

able	above	across	add	again	against	ago
air	almost	alone	along	already	also	although
always	am	American	among	animal	another	answer
any	anything	area	around	asked	away	back
ball	beautiful	became	because	become	before	began
begin	behind	below	best	better	between	black
blue	boat	body	book	both	bottom	box
boy	bring	brought	build	built	came	can't
Canada	car	care	carefully	carry	cat	center
centre	certain	change	check	children	city	class
close	common	complete	course	cut	dark	deep
didn't	different	distance	dog	don't	done	door
draw	dry	during	early	earth	easy	eat
either	else	end	English	enough	even	ever
every	everyone	everything	example	face	fact	fall
family	fast	feel	feet	felt	few	field
final	fine	fire	fish	five	floor	follow
food	foot	form	found	friend	front	full
fun	game	gave	get	girl	give	glass
going	gold	gone	good	got	great	green
ground	group	grow	half	hand	happen	hard
head	hear	heard	heart	heavy	held	help
high	himself	hold	home	horse	hot	hour
house	however	hundred	I'll	I'm	ice	idea
important	inside	instead	it's	itself	job	keep

Words I Can Read (2)
Next 365 Most Commonly Used Words (cont'd)

kept	kind	knew	land	language	large	last
later	lay	learn	learned	least	leave	leaves
left	less	letter	life	light	line	list
live	lived	living	longer	low	man	matter
mean	men	mixed	moon	morning	mother	move
much	must	near	need	never	new	nothing
notice	number	often	oh	old	once	open
order	our	outside	own	page	paper	part
past	pattern	perhaps	person	piece	place	plant
play	point	poor	possible	power	probably	problem
put	question	quite	rain	ran	read	ready
real	really	red	remember	rest	right	river
road	rock	room	round	run	sad	same
sat	school	sea	seen	sentence	set	several
shall	ship	short	should	show	side	simple
since	six	size	sky	small	snow	someone
something	sound	space	special	stand	start	state
stay	still	stood	stop	story	strong	such
suddenly	summer	sun	sure	system	table	take
talk	tall	tell	ten	that's	themselves	thing
think	third	those	though	thought	through	tiny
today	together	told	too	took	top	toward
town	tree	true	try	turn	turned	under
understand	until	upon	us	usually	voice	walk
walked	warm	watch	weather	well	whether	while
white	whole	why	wide	wild	wind	winter

NAME _____

Words I Can Read (2, 3)

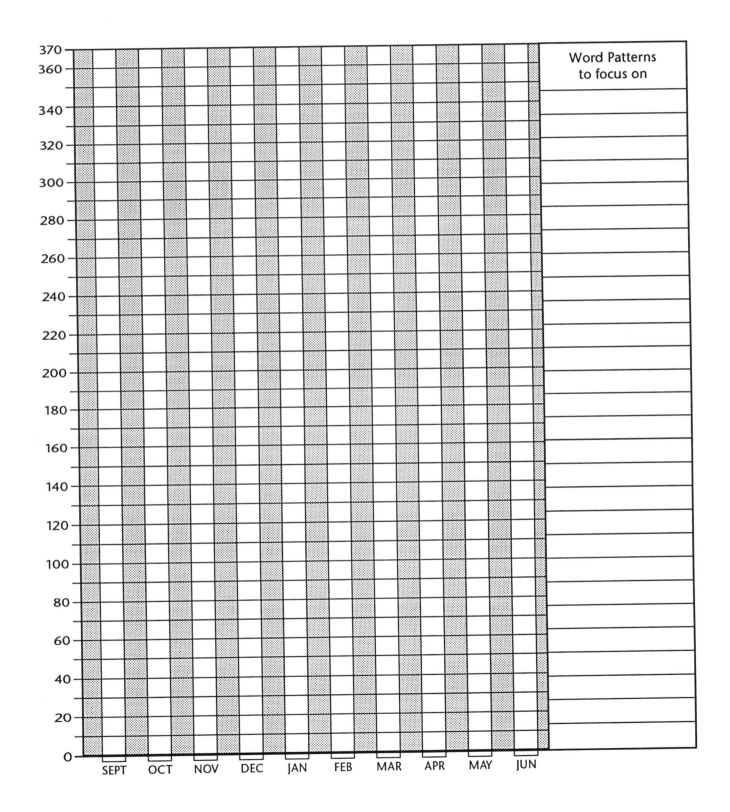

55

Word Recognition

Words I Can Read (4)
Next 564 Most Commonly Used Words

according	act	action	addition	afraid	afternoon	age
ahead	alive	amount	ancient	angry	anyone	apart
appear	arm	army	art	ate	attention	average
baby	bad	bag	band	bank	base	baseball
basic	bear	beat	bed	being	believe	beneath
beside	beyond	bird	bit	blood	blow	board
born	bottle	bought	bread	break	breakfast	breath
bright	broke	broken	brown	bus	business	busy
buy	cabin	cake	called	camp	cannot	capital
captain	case	catch	cattle	caught	cause	cent
centimetre	century	chair	chance	chart	cheque	chief
child	choose	church	circle	clean	clear	cloth
coal	coast	coat	cold	color	colour	column
community	company	compare	compound	consider	contain	control
cool	copy	corn	corner	correct	cost	cotton
couldn't	count	country	cover	cross	crowd	current
dance	danger	dead	deal	dear	death	decide
describe	desert	desk	develop	development	die	difference
difficult	dinner	direction	discover	divide	doctor	doesn't
double	Dr.	dress	drink	drive	drop	drove
dust	east	edge	effect	eight	electric	electricity
empty	energy	engine	enjoy	entire	equal	especially
evening	everybody	everywhere	except	exercise	expect	experience
experiment	explain	express	eye	fair	familiar	famous
far	farm	farmer	farther	fear	feed	fell

Words I Can Read (5)
Next 564 Most Commonly Used Words) (cont'd)

fence	fight	figure	fill	finger	finish	fit
flat	flew	flight	fly	fixed	force	forest
forth	forward	four	fourth	free	fresh	fruit
further	future	garden	gas	general	glad	government
grass	gray	grew	grown	guess	guide	gun
hair	happy	hat	he's	heat	herself	hill
history	hit	hole	hope	huge	human	hungry
hurt	I'd	I've	imagine	inch	include	indeed
industry	information	interest	iron	island	isn't	join
jump	key	kilometre	king	kitchen	knowledge	lady
laid	lake	late	law	lead	led	leg
length	let	level	lie	liquid	listen	litre
lost	lot	loud	machine	main	major	map
mark	market	mass	master	match	material	maybe
meant	measure	meat	meet	member	mental	met
method	metre	middle	mile	milk	million	mind
mine	minute	miss	modern	moment	money	month
motion	mountain	mouth	movement	Mr.	Mrs.	music
myself	narrow	nation	natural	nature	necessary	neck
neither	nest	next	nice	night	nine	noise
none	nor	north	northern	nose	note	noun
object	ocean	office	oil	onto	opposite	original
oxygen	paid	pair	paragraph	particular	party	pass
path	paw	pay	period	phrase	pick	picture
plain	plan	plane	please	poem	popular	population

Words I Can Read (6)
Next 564 Most Commonly Used Words (cont'd)

position	practice	present	pressure	pretty	process	produce
product	proper	protect	proud	provide	public	pull
purpose	push	quick	quiet	race	radio	raise
range	rate	rather	reach	reason	record	region
regular	report	represent	result	return	rich	ride
ring	rise	rode	root	rope	rose	row
rubber	rule	safe	salt	sand	scale	science
season	seat	second	section	seem	sell	send
sense	sent	separate	seven	shape	share	sharp
sheep	sheet	shook	shore	shot	shoulder	shown
sight	sign	silver	similar	sing	single	sit
skin	sleep	slow	soft	soil	sold	solid
solution	solve	son	song	soon	sort	soup
south	southern	speak	speech	speed	spend	spent
spoke	spot	spread	spring	square	stage	star
statement	station	steam	steel	step	stick	stone
store	storm	straight	strange	stream	street	strength
string	study	subject	sugar	supply	support	suppose
surprise	symbol	tail	teacher	team	teeth	television
temperature	tent	test	their	therefore	thick	thin
thousand	throughout	thus	till	time	tomorrow	total
touch	track	trade	train	travel	trip	trouble
truck	tube	twelve	twenty	twice	type	unit
United States	unless	use	useful	valley	value	variety
various	verb	village	visit	vowel	wagon	wait

Words I Can Read (4, 5, 6)
Next 564 Most Commonly Used Words

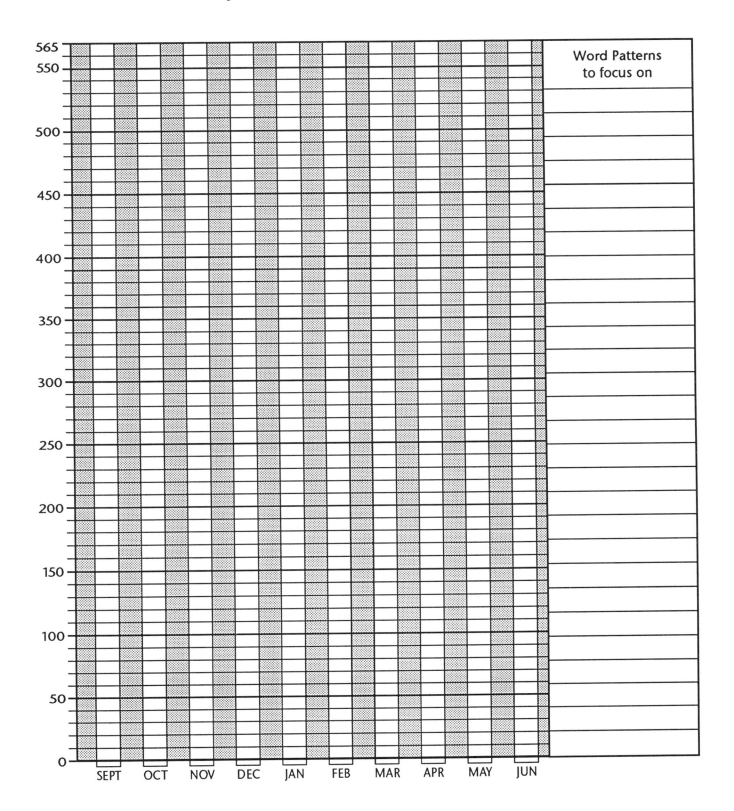

Word Patterns to focus on

Name _____

Words I am learning to read

Date _____

Words I am learning to read spell

Date _____

III. Examples

- **The student pages and portfolio progress records can be kept in a "pocket" portfolio, a duotang or a file folder.**

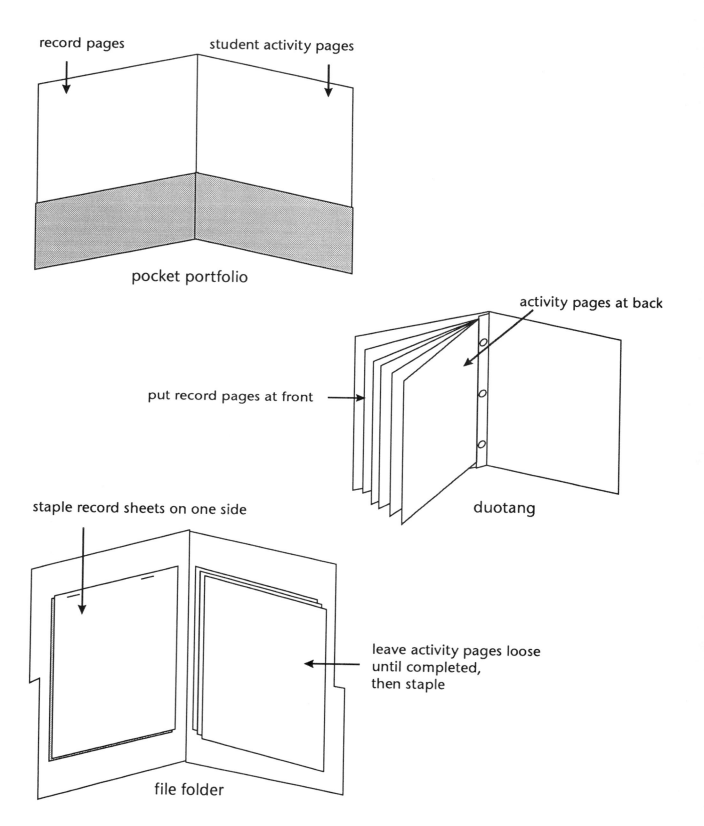

record pages   student activity pages

pocket portfolio

activity pages at back

put record pages at front

duotang

staple record sheets on one side

leave activity pages loose
until completed,
then staple

file folder

NAME **Emily**

Words I Can Read — A

* This is a portfolio progress record sheet, not used for teaching

a	come	here •	look	run	up
and	down	I	make	said	we
away	like •	in	me •	see	at
for •	is	my	the	yellow •	big
funny	it •	not	three •	you	blue •
go	jump	one •	to •	yes •	can
help	little	play •	two	this •	am •
good •	stop •				

Initial Assessment —

- *Words highlighted are those the student recognizes immediately (by sight, not sounded out). Students like to do their own highlighting.*

- *After initial assessment, words that are chosen to be learned are marked with a dot (•) to keep track of them. Those chosen are put on the activity pages and are focused on during reading sessions (see examples pp. 65-67).*

- *Those that are highlighted and have a dot indicate that they were ones learned after the initial assessment (e.g. Oct. 2) and highlighted during the following assessment times (e.g. in this sample, Oct. 26 or Nov. 5).*

- *Using different colours for highlighting each time also helps to show progress more clearly.*

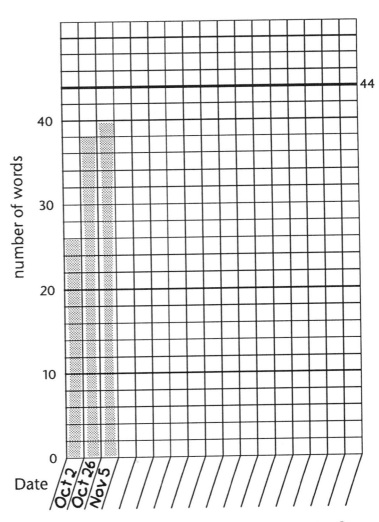

Words I Can Read — B

This is a portfolio progress record sheet, not used for teaching

all	did	must	ran	they	white
do	new	ride	who	are	eat
no	saw	too	will	ate	get
now	say	under	with	as	on
she	want	black	have	his	our
so	was	find	brown	he	out
soon	well	by	but	into	please
that	went	where	came	there	what

Initial Assessment —

• Words highlighted are those the student recognizes immediately (by sight, not sounded out). Students like to do their own highlighting.

• After initial assessment, words that are chosen to be learned are marked with a dot (•) to keep track of them. Those chosen are put on the activity pages and are focused on during reading sessions (see examples pp. 65-67).

• Those that are highlighted and have a dot indicate that they were ones learned after the initial assessment (e.g. Oct. 2) and highlighted during the following assessment times (e.g. in this sample, Oct. 26).

• Using different colours for highlighting each time also helps to show progress more clearly.

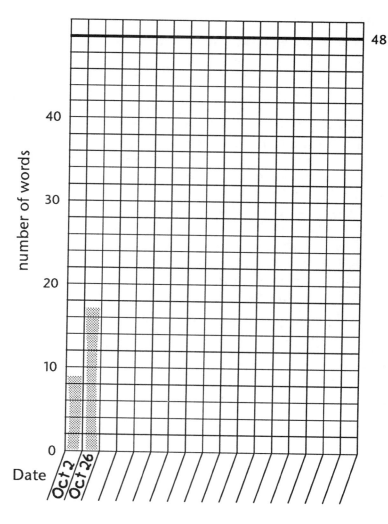

Words I am learning to read
Date _Oct 18_

In margins you can add words/word parts for teaching and extra focus on areas of difficulty – e.g. reversal of b & d for this student.

	Oct.	18	19	20	21	22	25	
away		√	√	√	√	√	√	
find		•	•	•	•	√	•	
me		√	√	√	√	√	√	
yellow		√	√	√	√	√	√	
three		•	√	•	•	√	•	
blue		√	√	√	√	√	√	
she		•	√	√	√	√	√	
did		•	√	√	√	√	√	

but
big
dad
dog
bad
bat

√   *Students check word themselves as they read word easily and correctly.*

•   *Students put dot if they still need to learn word.*

If student has not learned word easily (e.g. three), then this word may be added to new list.

My Stories

Student and teacher make up stories containing the words. Student can highlight words in passage. Each day they read passage first, then read words above.

She can see three yellow books.
Can she find the blue book?
I did not see the yellow book
or the red book or the blue book.
Three books are lost. I should
have put them away.

d b d
d b b
d b d
d d b

This activity is used for introducing words. It is important that student also reads other stories and notes these words in those stories.

As students are learning the "focus" words, they are also reading words in context and learning other words and strategies at the same time.

NAME **Emily**

Words I am learning to read

Date **Oct 27**

ent

wen̲t̲

t̲e̲n̲t̲

b̲e̲n̲t̲

s̲e̲n̲t̲

l̲e̲n̲t̲

do	✓	✓	✓	✓			
get	✓	✓	✓	✓			
all	•	•	•	✓			
saw	•	•	✓	✓			
this	✓	✓	✓	✓			
eat	•	✓	✓	✓			
he	✓	✓	✓	✓			
went	•	•	•	•			
Oct.	27	28	29	30			

p̲e̲n̲t̲

rent

✓   *Students check word themselves as they read word easily and correctly.*

•   *Students put dot if they still need to learn word.*

If student has not learned words easily (e.g. all, went), then these words may be added to new list.

My Stories

Student and teacher make up stories containing the words. Student can highlight words in passage. Each day they read passage first, then read words above.

all

ball

tall

fall

hall

wall

mall

Emily saw a cat eat some food he went to eat all this food but then he saw a mouse. Do you think he will eat this mouse? He will get fat, won't he?

This activity is used for introducing words. It is important that student also reads other stories and notes these words in those stories.

As students are learning the "focus" words, they are also reading words in context and learning other words and strategies at the same time.

NAME **James**

Words I am learning to read

Date **Nov. 3**

said	•	•	•	√	√		Where did she
here	√	√	√	√	√		find the three
find	•	•	√	√	√		black hats? "Over
where	•	•	√	•	√		here," said the witch.
three	√	•	√	√	√		So I went over to
as	√	√	√	√	√		see the three hats.
black	•	√	•	•	√		As I went, three
so	•	•	√	√	√		black cats ran away
Nov.	3	4	5	6	7		as fast as they could.

- *Student and teacher make up sentences containing the words. Then student can read sentences first before checking the words in the list.*

- *It is important for students to also read other material after this activity and to find these words in their reading.*

Words I am learning to (read) spell

Date **Nov. 10**

say						
went						
was						
that						
all						
now						
have						
saw						
Nov.	10	11				

Word Recognition

IV. Connecting with Spelling

Once children can easily recognize these words, they can begin to learn to spell them from memory.

Children can choose words themselves from their assessment page and print them on the activity page. During the week, they can practice with a buddy and at home. They can find the words in their reading and writing and discuss strategies for remembering the words.

You can also add words with phonic patterns from other language arts and theme studies in your classroom. In this way a more personalized spelling program can be developed in your class, at the same time as ensuring students are learning the most frequently used words and common phonetic patterns.

Words I Can Spell — A

a	come	I	make	see	we
am	down	in	me	stop	yellow
and	for	is	my	the	yes
at	funny	it	not	this	you
away	go	jump	one	to	
big	good	like	play	tree	
blue	help	little	run	two	
can	here	look	said	up	

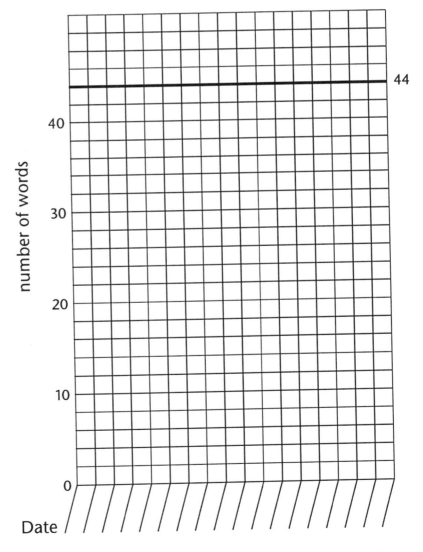

number of words

44

Date

Words I Can Spell — B

all	came	his	out	soon	well
are	did	into	please	that	went
as	do	must	ran	there	what
ate	eat	new	ride	they	where
black	find	no	saw	too	white
brown	get	now	say	under	who
but	have	on	she	want	will
by	he	our	so	was	with

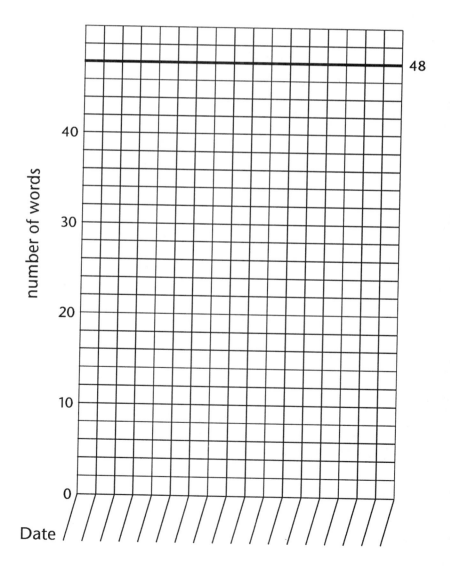

Words I Can Spell — C

after	every	her	may	put	them
again	fly	him	of	round	then
an	from	how	old	sit	think
any	give	just	open	sleep	us
ask	going	know	or	some	were
call	had	let	over	take	when
could	has	live	pretty	thank	

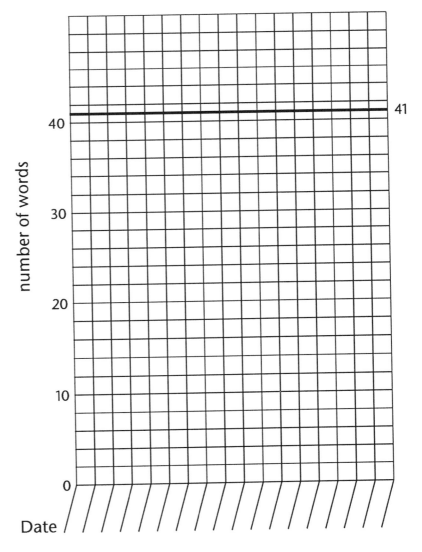

number of words

41

40

30

20

10

0

Date

Words I Can Spell — D

always	does	green	pull	those	work
around	don't	if	read	upon	would
because	fast	its	right	use	your
been	five	made	sing	very	
before	found	many	start	walk	
best	gave	off	tell	wash	
buy	goes	once	their	which	
cold	got	pick	these	wish	

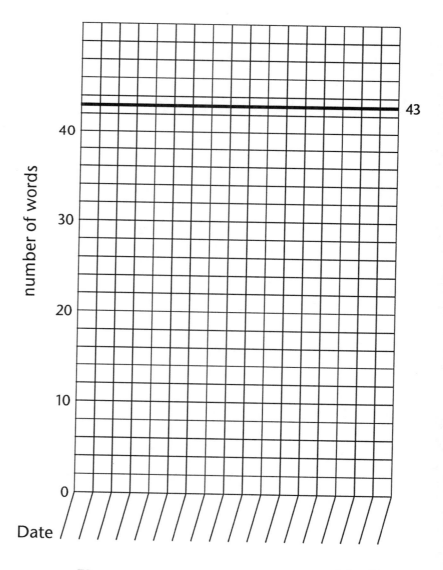

number of words

43

40

30

20

10

0

Date

Words I Can Spell — E

about	done	full	laugh	own	today
better	draw	grows	light	seven	together
both	drink	hold	long	shall	try
bring	eight	hot	much	show	warm
carry	fall	hurt	myself	six	why
clean	far	keep	never	small	write
cut	first	kind	only	ten	

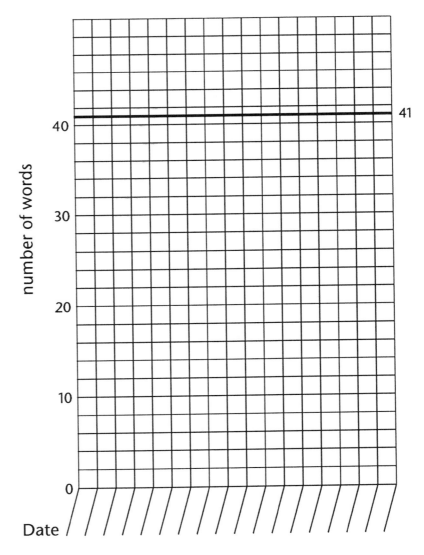

number of words

40 — 41

30

20

10

0

Date

Words I Can Spell (1)
(115 Most Commonly Used Words)

a	about	after	all	an	and	are
as	at	be	been	big	brother	but
by	can	come	could	dad	day	did
do	does	down	each	find	first	for
from	go	had	has	have	he	her
here	him	his	how	I	if	in
into	is	it	its	just	know	like
little	long	look	love	made	make	many
may	me	mom	more	most	my	name
no	not	now	of	off	on	one
only	or	other	out	over	people	said
saw	say	see	she	sister	so	some
than	that	the	them	then	there	these
they	this	three	to	two	up	very
want	was	way	we	went	were	what
when	where	which	who	will	with	would
yes	you	your				

Words I Can Spell (1)
115 Most Commonly Used Words

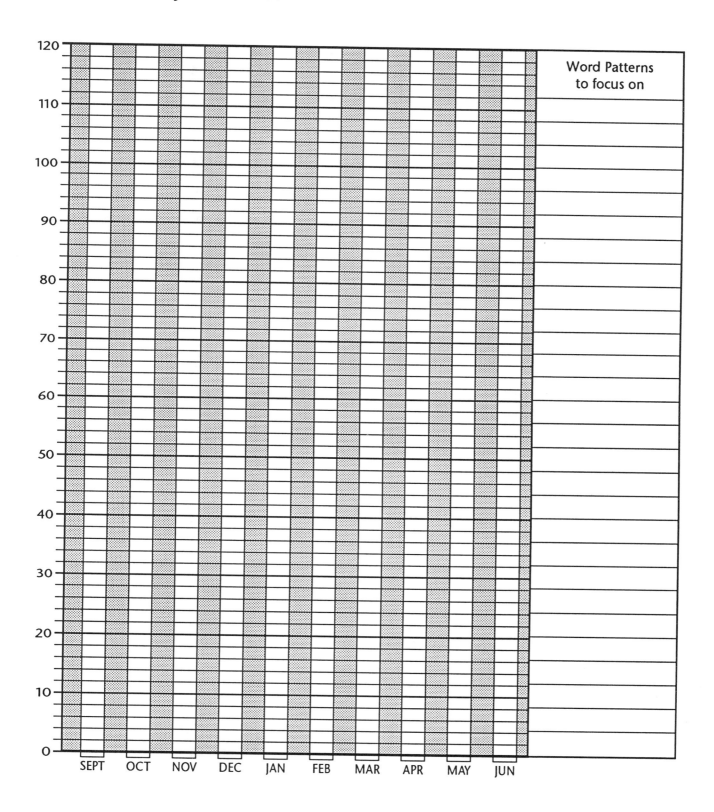

Words I Can Spell (2)
Next 365 Most Commonly Used Words

able	above	across	add	again	against	ago
air	almost	alone	along	already	also	although
always	am	American	among	animal	another	answer
any	anything	area	around	asked	away	back
ball	beautiful	became	because	become	before	began
begin	behind	below	best	better	between	black
blue	boat	body	book	both	bottom	box
boy	bring	brought	build	built	came	can't
Canada	car	care	carefully	carry	cat	center
centre	certain	change	check	children	city	class
close	common	complete	course	cut	dark	deep
didn't	different	distance	dog	don't	done	door
draw	dry	during	early	earth	easy	eat
either	else	end	English	enough	even	ever
every	everyone	everything	example	face	fact	fall
family	fast	feel	feet	felt	few	field
final	fine	fire	fish	five	floor	follow
food	foot	form	found	friend	front	full
fun	game	gave	get	girl	give	glass
going	gold	gone	good	got	great	green
ground	group	grow	half	hand	happen	hard
head	hear	heard	heart	heavy	held	help
high	himself	hold	home	hjorse	hot	hour
house	however	hundred	I'll	I'm	ice	idea
important	inside	instead	it's	itself	job	keep
kept	kind	knew	land	language	large	last

Words I Can Spell (3)
Next 365 Most Commonly Used Words (cont'd)

later	lay	learn	learned	least	leave	leaves
left	less	letter	life	light	line	list
live	lived	living	longer	low	man	matter
mean	men	mixed	moon	morning	mother	move
much	must	near	need	never	new	nothing
notice	number	often	oh	old	once	open
order	our	outside	own	page	paper	part
past	pattern	perhaps	person	piece	place	plant
play	point	poor	possible	power	probably	problem
put	question	quite	rain	ran	read	ready
real	really	red	remember	rest	right	river
road	rock	room	round	run	sad	same
sat	school	sea	seen	sentence	set	several
shall	ship	short	should	show	side	simple
since	six	size	sky	small	snow	someone
something	sound	space	special	stand	start	state
stay	still	stood	stop	story	strong	such
suddenly	summer	sun	sure	system	table	take
talk	tall	tell	ten	that's	themselves	thing
think	third	those	though	thought	through	tiny
today	together	told	too	took	top	toward
town	tree	true	try	turn	turned	under
understand	until	upon	us	usually	voice	walk
walked	warm	watch	weather	well	whether	while
white	whole	why	wide	wild	wind	winter
within	without	work	world	write	year	yet

Words I Can Spell (2, 3)

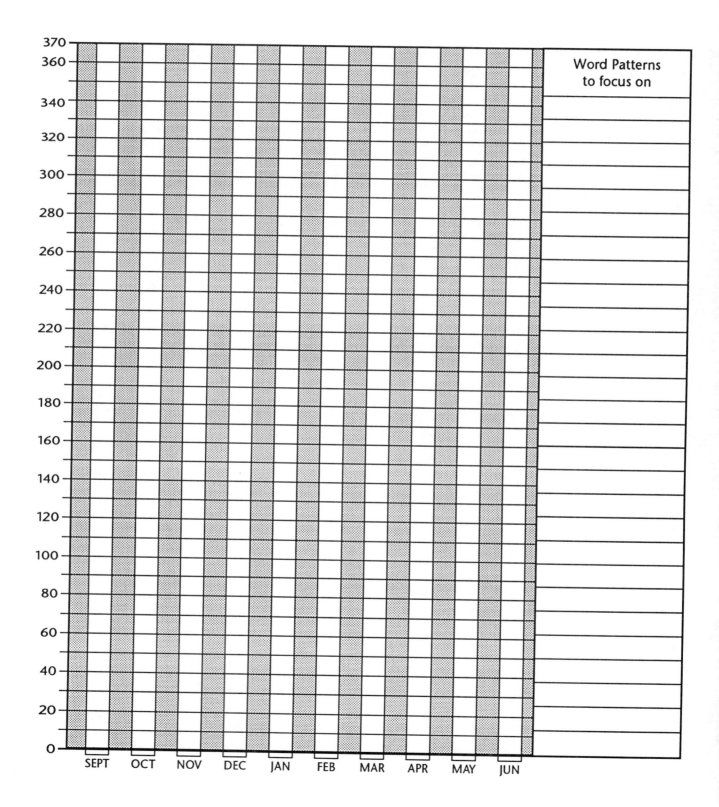

Words I Can Spell (4)
Next 564 Most Commonly Used Words

according	act	action	addition	afraid	afternoon	age
ahead	alive	amount	ancient	angry	anyone	apart
appear	arm	army	art	ate	attention	average
baby	bad	bag	band	bank	base	baseball
basic	bear	beat	bed	being	believe	beneath
beside	beyond	bird	bit	blood	blow	board
born	bottle	bought	bread	break	breakfast	breath
bright	broke	broken	brown	bus	business	busy
buy	cabin	cake	called	camp	cannot	capital
captain	case	catch	cattle	caught	cause	cent
centimetre	century	chair	chance	chart	cheque	chief
child	choose	church	circle	clean	clear	cloth
coal	coast	coat	cold	color	colour	column
community	company	compare	compound	consider	contain	control
cool	copy	corn	corner	correct	cost	cotton
couldn't	count	country	cover	cross	crowd	current
dance	danger	dead	deal	dear	death	decide
describe	desert	desk	develop	development	die	difference
difficult	dinner	direction	discover	divide	doctor	doesn't
double	Dr.	dress	drink	drive	drop	drove
dust	east	edge	effect	eight	electric	electricity
empty	energy	engine	enjoy	entire	equal	especially
evening	everybody	everywhere	except	exercise	expect	experience
experiment	explain	express	eye	fair	familiar	famous
far	farm	farmer	farther	fear	feed	fell

Words I Can Spell (5)
Next 564 Most Commonly Used Words (cont'd)

fence	fight	figure	fill	finger	finish	fit
flat	flew	flight	fly	fixed	force	forest
forth	forward	four	fourth	free	fresh	fruit
further	future	garden	gas	general	glad	government
grass	gray	grew	grown	guess	guide	gun
hair	happy	hat	he's	heat	herself	hill
history	hit	hole	hope	huge	human	hungry
hurt	I'd	I've	imagine	inch	include	indeed
industry	information	interest	iron	island	isn't	join
jump	key	kilometre	king	kitchen	knowledge	lady
laid	lake	late	law	lead	led	leg
length	let	level	lie	liquid	listen	litre
lost	lot	loud	machine	main	major	map
mark	market	mass	master	match	material	maybe
meant	measure	meat	meet	member	mental	met
method	metre	middle	mile	milk	million	mind
mine	minute	miss	modern	moment	money	month
motion	mountain	mouth	movement	Mr.	Mrs.	music
myself	narrow	nation	natural	nature	necessary	neck
neither	nest	next	nice	night	nine	noise
none	nor	north	northern	nose	note	noun
object	ocean	office	oil	onto	opposite	original
oxygen	paid	pair	paragraph	particular	party	pass
path	paw	pay	period	phrase	pick	picture
plain	plan	plane	please	poem	popular	population

Words I Can Spell (6)
Next 564 Most Commonly Used Words (cont'd)

position	practice	present	pressure	pretty	process	produce
product	proper	protect	proud	provide	public	pull
purpose	push	quick	quiet	race	radio	raise
range	rate	rather	reach	reason	record	region
regular	report	represent	result	return	rich	ride
ring	rise	rode	root	rope	rose	row
rubber	rule	safe	salt	sand	scale	science
season	seat	second	section	seem	sell	send
sense	sent	separate	seven	shape	share	sharp
sheep	sheet	shook	shore	shot	shoulder	shown
sight	sign	silver	similar	sing	single	sit
skin	sleep	slow	soft	soil	sold	solid
solution	solve	son	song	soon	sort	soup
south	southern	speak	speech	speed	spend	spent
spoke	spot	spread	spring	square	stage	star
statement	station	steam	steel	step	stick	stone
store	storm	straight	strange	stream	street	strength
string	study	subject	sugar	supply	support	suppose
surprise	symbol	tail	teacher	team	teeth	television
temperature	tent	test	their	therefore	thick	thin
thousand	throughout	thus	till	time	tomorrow	total
touch	track	trade	train	travel	trip	trouble
truck	tube	twelve	twenty	twice	type	unit
United States	unless	use	useful	valley	value	variety
various	verb	village	visit	vowel	wagon	wait

Words I Can Spell (4, 5, 6)
Next 564 Most Commonly Used Words

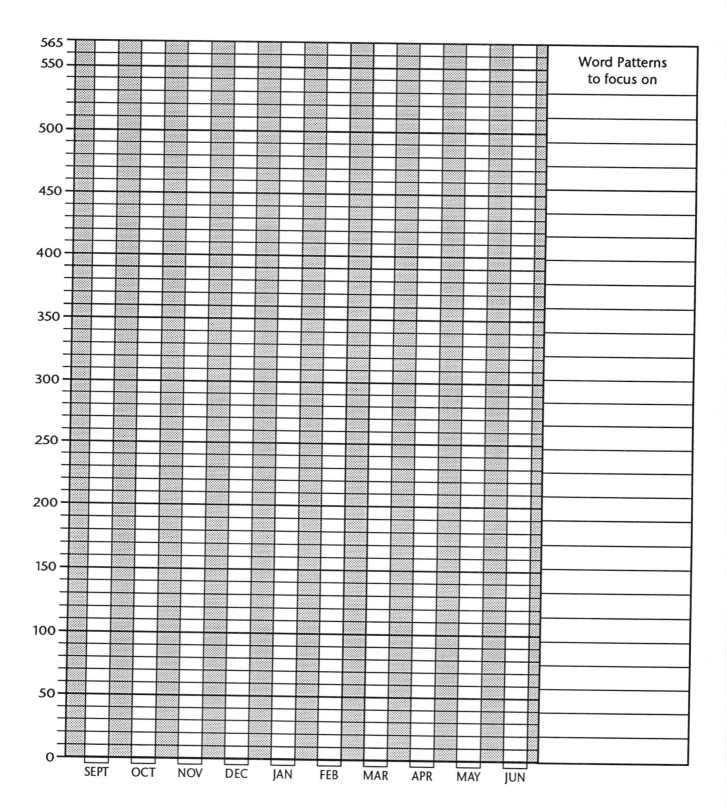

Word Patterns to focus on

SEPT   OCT   NOV   DEC   JAN   FEB   MAR   APR   MAY   JUN

Words I am learning to read

Words I am learning to spell

Words I am learning to spell

Words I am learning to spell

Date _____
